STEP ONE: TEACH YOURSELF DRUMS

DVD Edition

T0080131

Cover photography by Randall Wallace

This book Copyright © 2004 by Amsco Publications,
A Division of Music Sales Corporation, New York

Order No. AM 974303
US International Standard Book Number: 0.8256.1958.0
UK International Standard Book Number: 0.7119.9468.4

Exclusive Distributors:
Music Sales Corporation
257 Park Avenue South, New York, NY 10010 USA
Music Sales Limited
8/9 Frith Street, London W1D 3JB England
Music Sales Pty. Limited
120 Rothschild Street, Rosebery, Sydney, NSW 2018, Australia

Printed in the United States of America by
Vicks Lithograph and Printing Corporation

Amsco Publications
New York/London/Paris/Sydney/Copenhagen/Berlin/Tokyo/Madrid

Contents

Introduction

Drums are among the few instruments you can begin to learn on your own, without a teacher. Since drums are non-pitched instruments, you don't necessarily have to be concerned with knowing the names of the various pitches, or how to read and finger them on your instrument. And you don't have to worry about achieving a good tone or playing in tune—not sharp or flat. Drum music is based solely on rhythm, and only an elementary knowledge of rhythm is required for you to understand the rock beats in this book. The beats are all made up of quarter notes, eighth notes, sixteenth notes, and equivalent rests. You probably have at least some idea of these rhythms, but they will be explained. Clapping exercises are included so that you can gain a better working knowledge of how these rhythms sound.

Obviously, this self-teaching method can take you only so far. It can show you how to play the various rock beats in order to keep time with a band. And for most music, keeping time is the name of the game. That's the main function of drummers—not speeding up or slowing down. Just how well you play the beats and keep time depends on several different factors—how much you practice, how good your ear is, how much music you listen to, and how much experience you're able to get actually playing in a band. If, by the end of this book you decide you want to go further in developing your drumming skills, I suggest you take lessons from a competent teacher. Your local music dealer should be able to recommend a teacher; or an instructor in the music department of any school may be able to direct you to an appropriate person.

Before we get started learning rhythm or rock beats, a few words about the kit are in order. I will assume that you already own a set, or have access to one so that you can practice.

The Drum Seat

You should be able to adjust your drum seat, or "throne" as it is sometimes called, to various heights. Experiment with placing the seat in different positions to see how you feel the most comfortable. Various heights give you a different perception of the kit as a whole, and it may take months before you arrive at a fixed height at which you're comfortable.

I might mention that drummers tend to have bad posture when they play because they invariably hunch over in order to strike the various cymbals and drums. Backache and pain are common complaints, and these may often be avoided simply by sitting on a comfortable seat, adjusted to an appropriate height for your body. If you find you are having backache problems, try moving the seat to a different height and see what happens.

Tuning Your Drums

Drums are generally manufactured with top and bottom heads. Rock players, however, often remove the bottom heads from their tom toms to achieve the desired tone. In this case you only have to contend with tuning the top head. As with all tuning (indeed, with most aspects of playing), there is no right or wrong, but simply a matter of personal preference. If you want a high-pitched tom tom sound with a fast rebound of the stick, keep the drumhead taut. If, on the other hand, you want a deeper tone with a slower rebound, you will have to loosen the heads somewhat. Obviously, a problem arises if you want a deeper tone with a fast rebound for your stick. Well, you can't have both, so you simply must make a choice as to which is more important to you, then tighten the drumhead accordingly.

If you find you have too much overtone, fold some tissue into a little pad and tape it to the drumhead away from the playing area struck by your sticks. You can tape a handkerchief or any other piece of cloth to achieve the same results. If you know about pitches, you might try tuning your tom toms a fifth apart.

The Bass Drum

The players I know usually remove the front head from their bass drum and insert a pillow in order to get the sound they want. I prefer using a flat beater on my pedal because that also seems to help provide the desired sound.

The Snare Drum

This is the one drum that remains with both heads attached to the shell, or it wouldn't be able to produce its distinctive snare sound. Tighten the top head for action so that it gives you the rebound you seek. Then tighten the bottom head for tone. Try to get an even sound around the entire head. In order to do this it's best to tighten opposite lugs rather than adjacent ones. This method of tightening lugs ensures equal tension at all points on the snare, which helps to guarantee an equal sound.

Choosing Drum Sticks

Sticks come in hundreds of different sizes, as well as shapes. As a general rule I try to practice with the same sticks I use to play. However, many drummers use a heavier stick for practicing. Regardless of which size stick you use, try to be certain they are not warped. This is easily done by rolling them on a flat surface. If they wobble it means they're warped, so look for another pair. Also, tap the sticks on the counter and listen to their pitch. Try to pick a pair with the same pitch, which means the wood is the same weight and density.

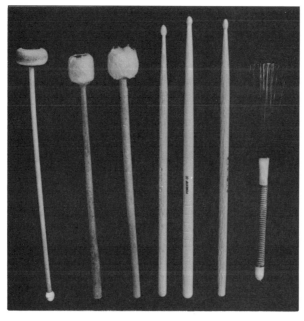

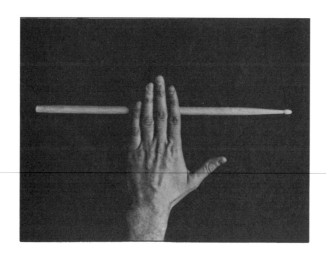

Quarter Notes

The *quarter note* looks like a large black dot, with a *stem* attached. The dot is called a *notehead,* and the stem may face up or down.

For a short time, forget about playing at your kit. Simply clap the following exercise and count as you clap—1, 2, 3, 4.

count: 1   2   3   4

You have just played one *bar* of rhythm. Some people call a bar a *measure,* and either term is acceptable.

Various bars of rhythm are separated by thin short lines called *barlines.*

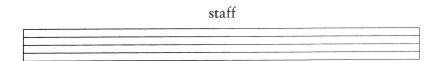

barlines

Music is written on a five-line *staff,* with each line and each space on the staff representing a specific pitch.

staff

Traditionally, music for the drum kit is written on a five-line staff. However, since drum kits are not usually tuned to a specific pitch there's no real reason to use a five-line staff. Indeed, much of the music you might see for drums, especially in tuition books, is written on a one-line staff. Two, three, and four lines are also used, with each line signifying a particular cymbal or drum. The beats and exercises in this book will be written on one or two lines.

Notice that in the next example the fraction $\frac{4}{4}$ appears just to the left of the bar. This fraction is called the *time signature.*

There are any number of possible time signatures such as $\frac{3}{4}$, $\frac{5}{4}$, $\frac{7}{4}$, $\frac{3}{8}$, $\frac{6}{8}$—but $\frac{4}{4}$ is the most common time signature used in rock music. In fact, $\frac{4}{4}$ is referred to as "common time," and may be indicated by the symbol ℂ.

In a time signature the top number of the fraction tells you how many beats there will be to a bar, while the bottom number tells you what kind of note will get one beat.

Quarter Rests

You've seen what a quarter note looks like, and this is the indication for a *quarter rest:*

Just as the name implies, a rest is not to be played. The following exercises contain quarter notes and quarter rests. Clap the exercises counting out loud 1, 2, 3, 4. Do not clap where you see a rest.

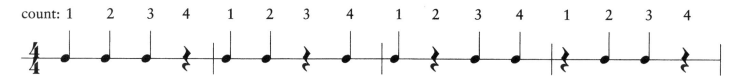

Eighth Notes

A *eighth note* looks just like a quarter note, but it has a *flag* hanging from the tip of the stem.

In arithmetic two eighths equal a quarter ($\frac{1}{8} + \frac{1}{8} = \frac{1}{4}$). In music, two eighth notes equal a quarter note.

When you see groups of eighth notes, they are often connected by a *beam* instead of having their own individual flags.

Clap the following exercise. The eighth notes must be played twice as fast as the quarter notes.

The plus sign over the second quaver means that you should say "and."

When a composer wants a portion of music played over again, he or she will write a repeat sign which looks like this:

Clapping Quarter Notes and Eighth Notes

Clap the following bars of rhythm over and over until they can be played smoothly, without hesitation.

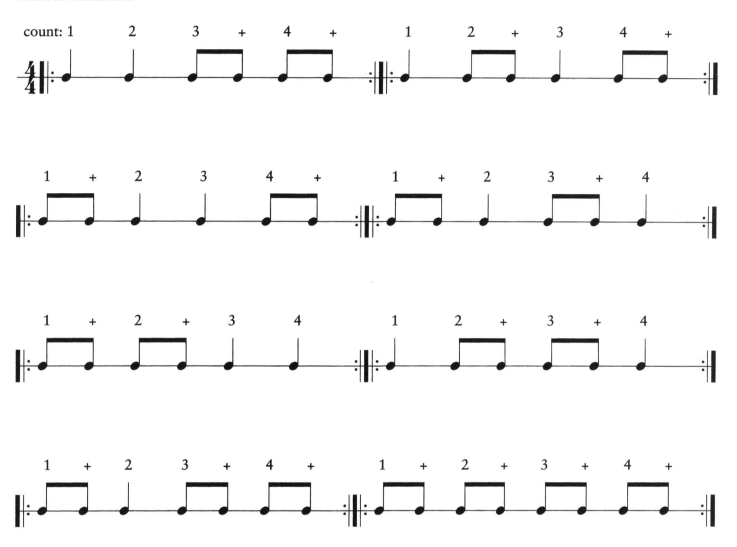

Two Possible Rock Band Set Ups

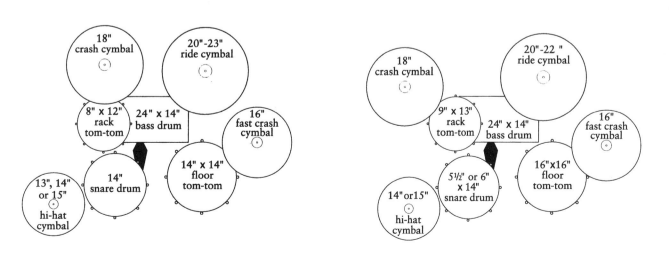

Sitting at the Kit

You're now ready to sit at the kit and learn the basic rock rhythms. The following pictures illustrate the position of the hi-hat (sock cymbals) and the bass drum.

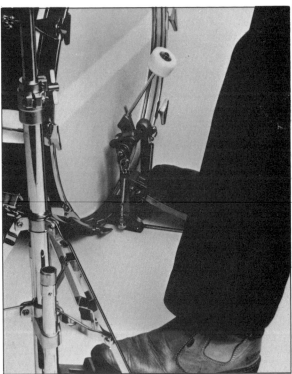

Notice the hi-hat is controlled by your left foot, while the right foot rests on the bass drum pedal. I'm assuming you're right-handed. If you happen to be left-handed, set up your kit in reverse. Do not try to play like a right-handed drummer.

Holding the Sticks

There are several ways to hold the sticks, but the grip used by most rock players is the "matched grip," and it's the one I suggest you use. An easy and natural way to grasp sticks, it creates the fewest problems for beginners. Hold the drumstick firmly between your thumb and index finger. Now place the three remaining fingers under and around the stick. Your palms should be facing down. This grip is the same in each hand.

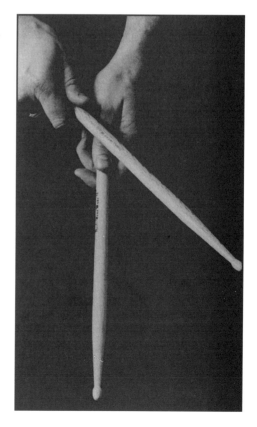

When you play, try to keep your arms fairly steady, moving the sticks mainly from your wrists. Too much arm motion can create a strain in the muscles, hampering your ability to play with speed and control.

Rockin' Hi-Hat Rhythm

In rock drumming the right stick plays mostly on the hi-hat, which is often in a closed position. You keep the cymbals closed by depressing the pedal of the hi-hat. The disco sound is produced by opening and closing the cymbals, but I'll talk about that later in the book.

Now, with your right stick tap the following rhythm on the closed hi-hat, repeating it over and over until it can be played with smoothness and ease.

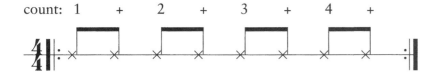

As you can see, **X**s were used as noteheads instead of dots. In drum music, **X**s are generally used to denote the cymbal rhythm.

This next exercise shows you when to strike the snare drum with your left stick.

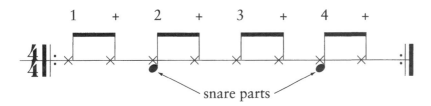

Notice that the hi-hat rhythm is played continually, while the left stick strikes the snare only on the counts of two and four. This is the simplest, most basic pattern in rock drumming.

Elementary Rock Beats

The following group of exercises shows various possibilities for playing the bass drum, while the hi-hat and snare drum are played exactly as indicated in the last exercise.

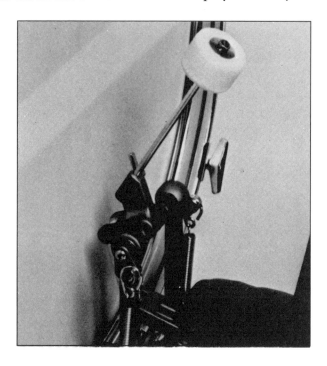 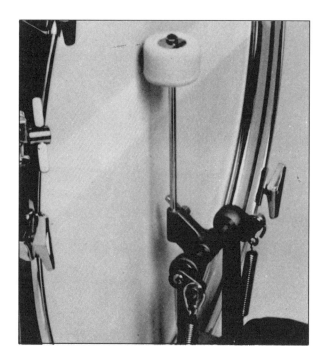

Notes for the bass drum have their stems facing down, and the staff will now include a second line specifically for the bass drum part.

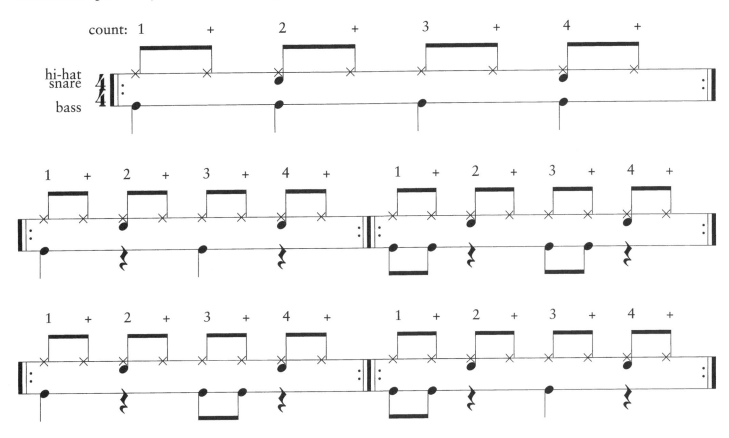

Armed with the previous five beats, you can play with a rock group. It's true—all you have to do is be able to play each of the beats above without speeding up or slowing down and you can join a band. In fact, the first and second beat is sufficient for you to keep time with a little rock group. They will fit at least seventy-five percent of the rock music you hear.

Eighth-Note Rests

It's time to move along and learn more variations for the bass drum. In order to do this you must understand the *eighth rest* which looks like this:

Here are a few exercises to clap. They incorporate eighth rests at various positions in the bar. **Remember:** Count out loud, and do not clap when you come to a rest.

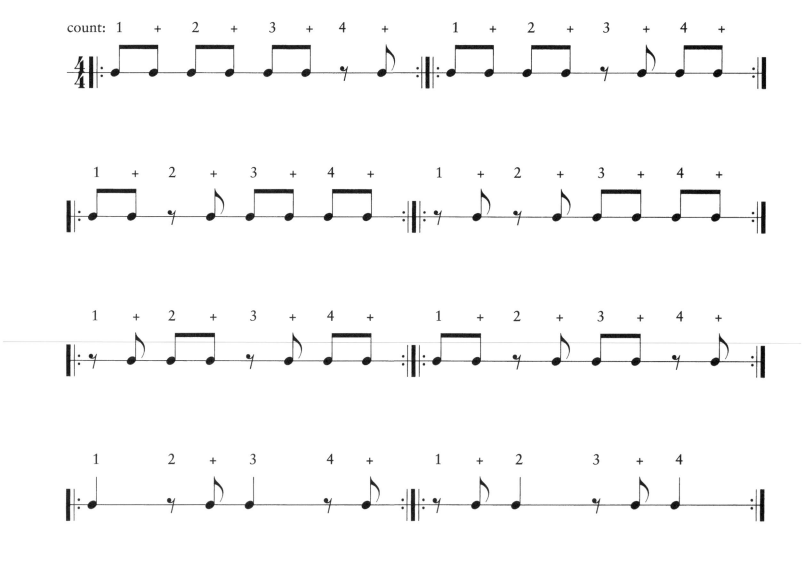

Rockin' Bass-Drum Variations

The following beats are all variations for the bass drum involving eighth rests. The hi-hat part remains the same as always—you tap continual eighth notes on the cymbals (which are locked together), while the snare is played on the counts of two and four. Being well coordinated with the bass drum is at the heart (or should I say the "soul") of rock drumming, and these exercises will help develop your ability to play different beats with quarter notes and eighth notes.

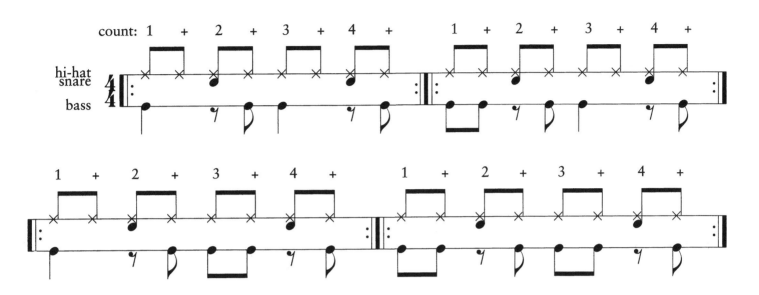

The first exercise is the most commonly used beat in rock drumming.

More Bass-Drum Variations

Offbeat Bass Drum

The previous beats all contained a bass drum on the first beat of the bar. The following variations may prove a little trickier because there is no bass drum on the count of one.

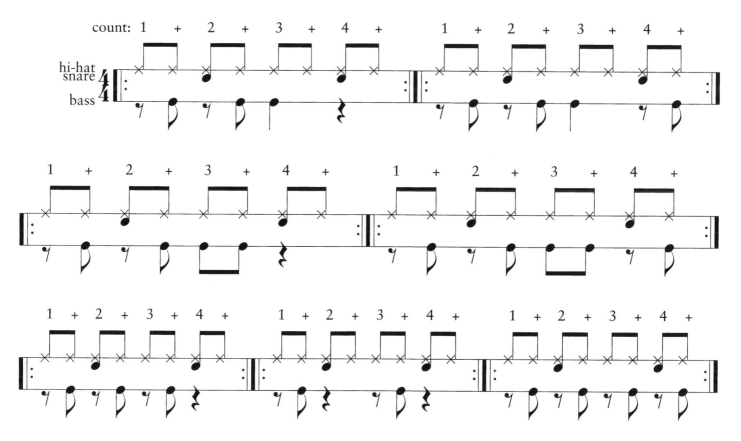

Two-Measure Rock Beats

Until now, all the beats have been for one bar. The following beats are two-bar patterns. In other words, each exercise will be two bars long. A great deal of rock music is phrased with a two-bar feel.

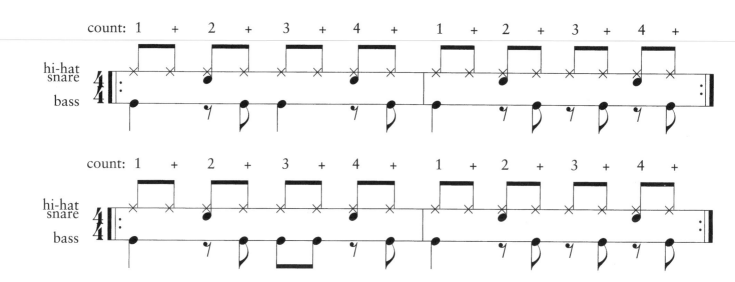

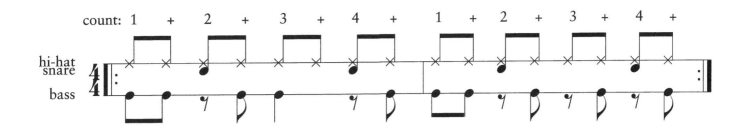

More Two-Measure Rock Beats

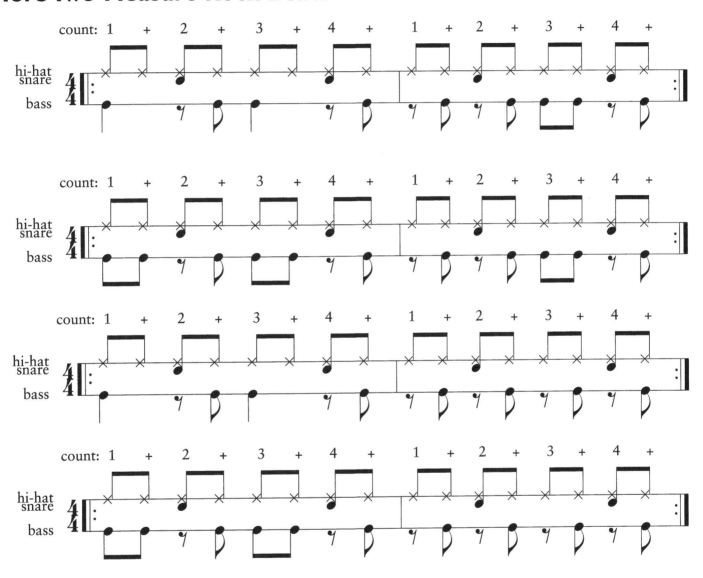

Basic Rock Beats with Snare-Drum Variations

So far the snare drum has been played only on the counts of two and four. The following one-bar exercises will show some simple variations. At first these variations are shown without a bass-drum part, but the bass will be included on the subsequent pages.

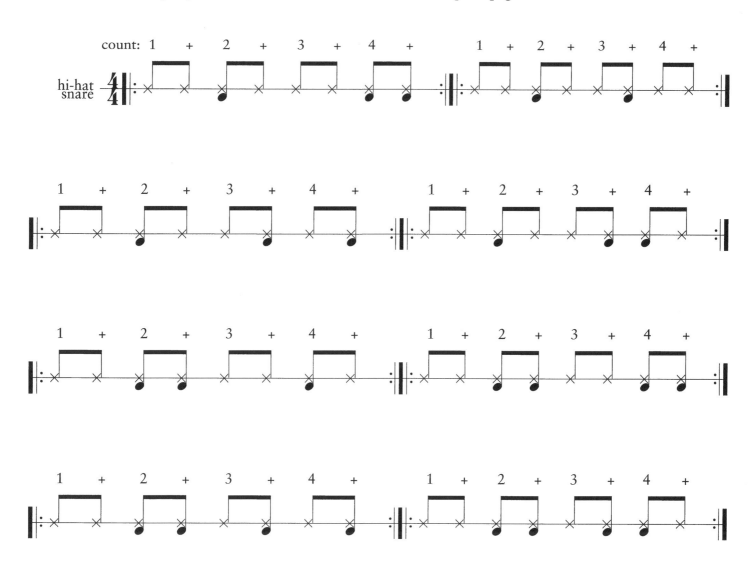

More Snare-Drum Variations

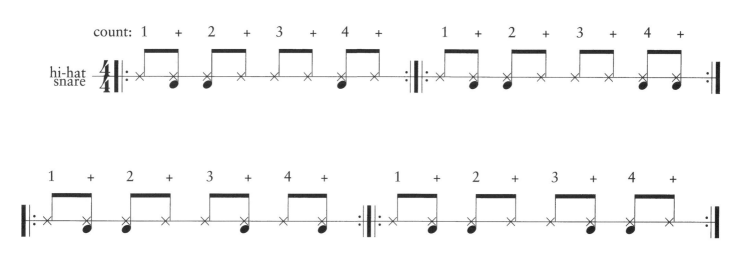

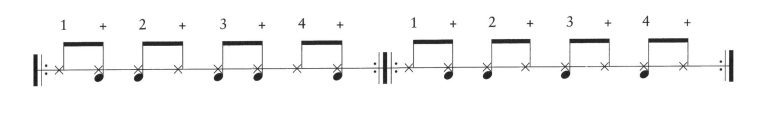

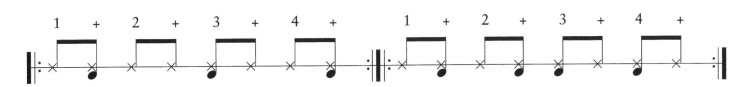

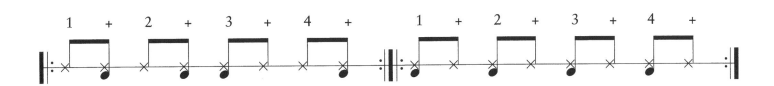

The next examples show snare-drum variations with a bass-drum part included.

Bossa Nova Rock Beats

The Bossa Nova is a basic Latin rhythm which is sometimes applied to rock music. The snare is played with your left hand across the face of the drumhead and over the rim, giving a "click" sound. The beat is phrased over two bars, so be certain to repeat the beat as two-bar patterns. Notice that the snare part is not played simply on two and four.

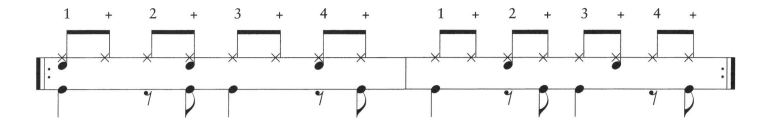

Disco Rock Beats

Until now, the hi-hat part has been played with the cymbals locked together. The sound of the disco beat involves opening and closing the cymbals at various spots. These next two pages will focus upon opening and closing the hi-hat on offbeats. The snare part is played simply on the counts of two and four, while the bass drum is played on every downbeat.

Important: The letter "o" above a note means that the hi-hat cymbals should be opened on that note, and that note alone. Be certain to keep your hi-hat cymbals together on all other notes.

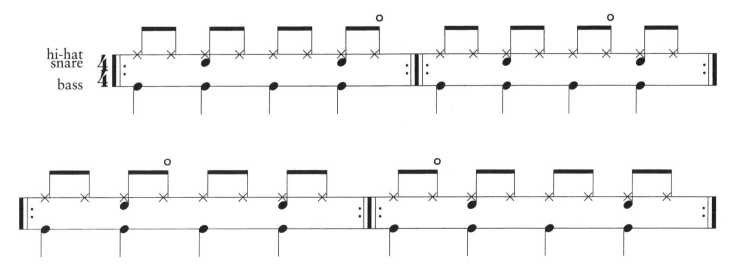

More Disco Beats

Jazz Rock Beats

Back in the fifties when rock music first emerged, beats were based upon a jazz feel. And even today rock drummers sometimes find themselves having to play a basic jazz beat, which is based upon eighth-note triplets. In other words there are three eighth-notes to a beat.

Here are some clapping exercises with eighth-note triplets.

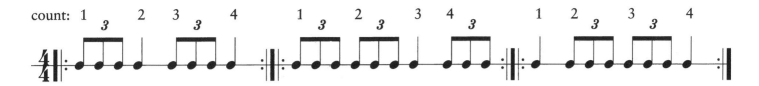

The actual jazz or jazz rock cymbal rhythm has the middle eighth note omitted, which gives a kind of skip feel to the rhythm. In fact, it might be helpful if you used the word "skip" in your count.

Jazz Rock Cymbal Rhythm

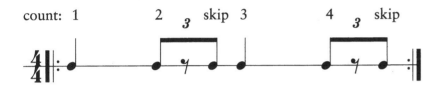

Play the following jazz rock beats which include the snare drum on two and four, as well as bass drum variations.

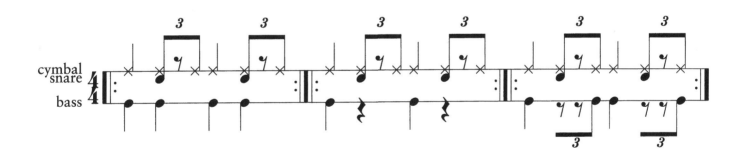

Gospel Rock Beats

The beats on the previous pages have all been in $\frac{4}{4}$ time. A certain amount of rock music, however, is played with a $\frac{12}{8}$ feel, which means there are twelve eighth-notes in every bar and each eighth note gets a beat. Understanding the precise meaning of a time signature might be a little confusing, but the exercises are easy to play. Notice that the twelve eighth-notes are grouped in threes. Since each eighth note gets a beat, you might count 1, 2, 3, 4, 5, 6, 7, 8, 9, 10, 11, 12. However, that can prove a little wordy, so I suggest you count as indicated: 1, 2, 3, 1, 2, 3, 1, 2, 3, 1, 2, 3.

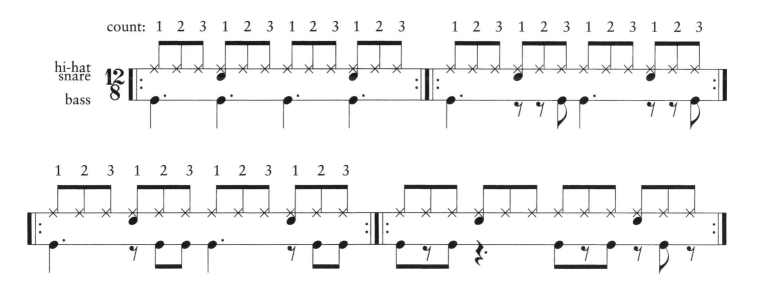

Shuffle Rock Beats

The shuffle is another feel that is commonly heard in rock music, and it is closely related to the jazz beat because the shuffle rhythm is based upon eighth note triplets with the middle triplet omitted. Here's the basic cymbal rhythm by itself.

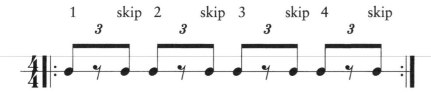

The following five beats include bass drum variations, with the snare part being played on the counts of two and four, as usual.

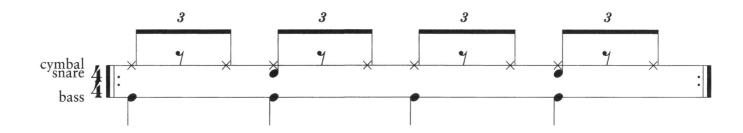

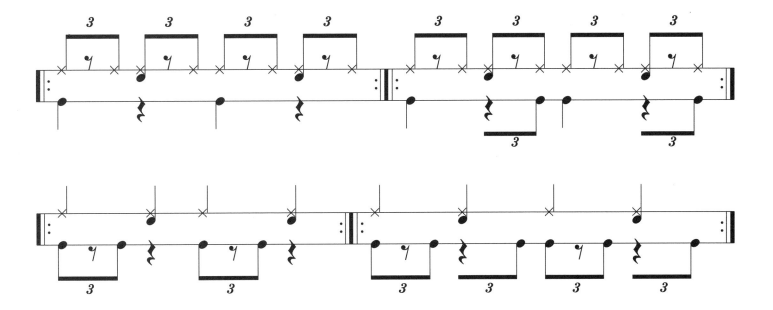

Notice that in the last two beats the skip feel is played on the bass rather than the cymbal.

At this point you might well ask, "Just what beat should I use?" The question is reasonable enough, but the answer is not so simple. In fact there's no definite answer because you don't necessarily play one beat throughout a song. In most instances a drummer falls into playing a pattern that fits the tune, breaking away from that pattern every once in a while in order to accent certain portions of the music with the band. You can never go wrong by keeping steady time and playing simply. However, if you're capable of coordinating your bass drum with different rhythmic variations, then by all means do so. In short, you can play whatever you feel as long as it fits the music, and as long as no one else in the band objects. A good idea is to work closely with the bass player so that your bass drum variations are similar to the rhythm that he's playing on his electric bass. You could, of course, work out patterns that are exactly what the bass player is playing.

If you're not actually in a band, practice along with records or tapes. Turn the volume up as much as possible so that you're engulfed by sound. Fantasize that you are the drummer with the band on the recording. If you have nervous neighbors (or parents) you'll have to tone it down, but playing along with tapes and records is the best way I know to develop your ear in order to play with a band.

Sixteenth Notes

You have now reached a point where the possibilities for playing rock beats with quarter notes and eighth notes have been explored to the limits of this book. In order to go further you must be able to play the next subdivision of rhythm—sixteenth notes.

The *sixteenth note* looks just like a eighth note, but it has an extra flag on its stem:

Each eighth note equals two sixteenth-notes (♪=♬) so four sixteenth-notes are equivalent to one quarter-note.

♬♬ = ♩

When sixteenth notes are grouped together, it's common to see them joined with two beams.

The following clapping exercises will help you gain a better working knowledge of sixteenth notes, which is absolutely necessary for understanding the subsequent rock beats. Remember that four sixteenth-notes have to be clapped in the time of one quarter-note. Maintain a slow and steady tempo, counting out loud as indicated.

Clapping Sixteenth Notes

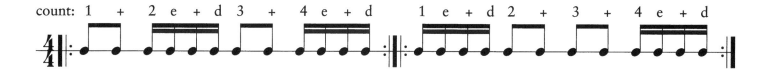

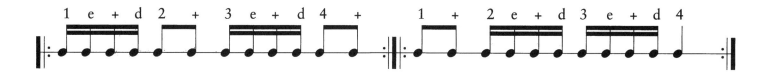

More Clapping Exercises

The next series of clapping exercises combine eighth notes and sixteenth notes. Featured first is the following rhythm:

Notice the relationship between these three notes and four consecutive sixteenth notes.

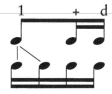

Clap the exercises at a steady tempo, and count as indicated.

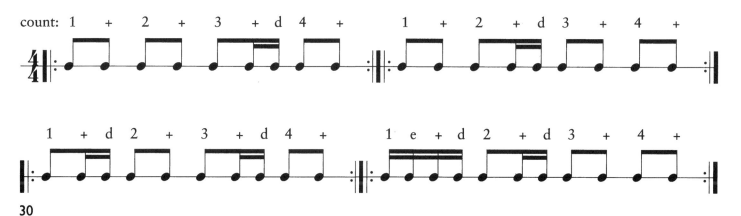

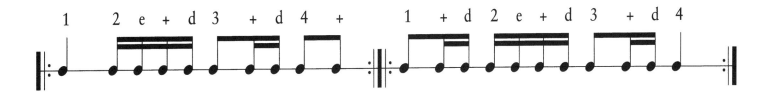

Featured below is the reverse rhythm:

The sixteenth notes now begin on the beat rather than on the offbeat, and this is how it lines up with consecutive sixteenth notes.

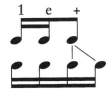

Clap the following exercises.

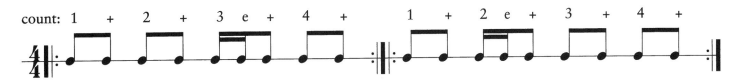

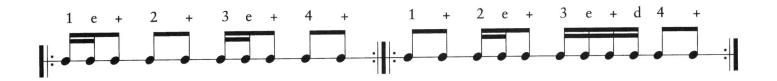

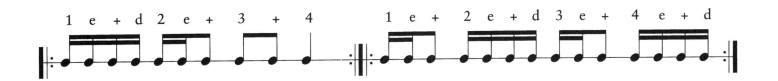

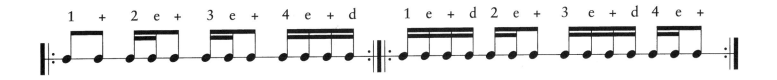

The clapping exercises on this page combine the rhythms from the previous pages.

Sixteenth-Note Variations for Snare Drum

Now we can move right along and learn some variations for snare drum that include sixteenth notes. This first set of exercises will show the variations without a bass drum part. The next set will include a part for the bass.

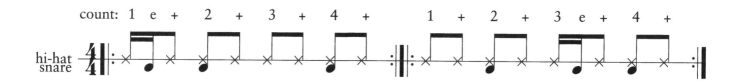

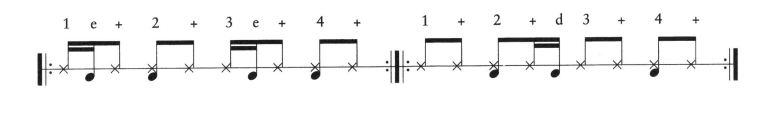

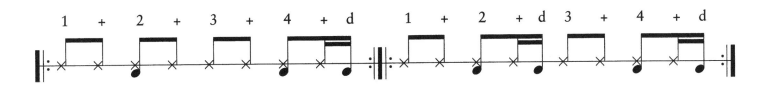

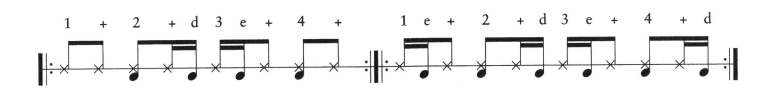

The following exercises demonstrate snare drum variations with, and a simple bass part is included.

Sixteenth-Note Variations for Bass Drum

So far the variations with sixteenth notes have all been played on the snare drum. The following few pages will demonstrate sixteenth-note variations for the bass, while the snare is played on two and four. The rhythms for bass drum will contain *sixteenth rests,* which look like this:

Although these rhythms may look a little unfamiliar, the bass drum part is lined up exactly with the hi-hat part, so you should be able to determine exactly when to strike the bass.

More Sixteenth-Note Variations for Bass Drum

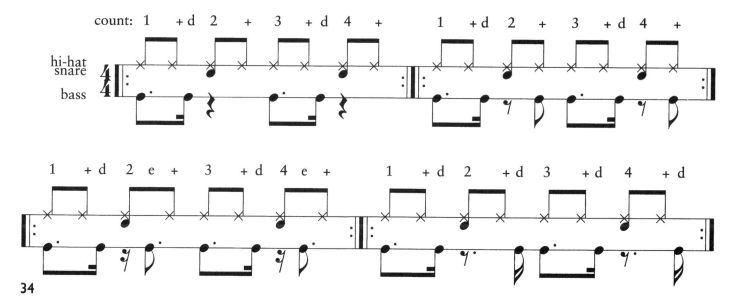

The beats below are combinations of sixteenth notes between the bass drum and snare.

Offbeat Snare Drum

Until now, the snare has been played on the counts of two and four, or with sixteenth note variations. This one page demonstrates some useful bass drum patterns with the snare played simply on offbeats.

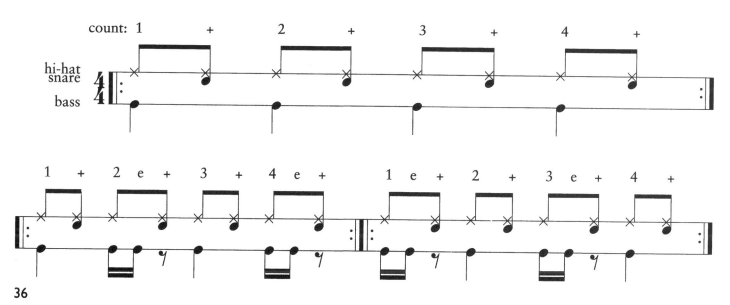

Blues Rock Beats

Since you now know some beats involving sixteenth notes, it would be a good idea to double back and play some more variations with a 12/8 feel using sixteenth notes. These beats are good for gospel music and slow-tempo blues, which are usually played in twelve-bar phrases.

Rock Beats for Slow Tempos

A great deal of rock in $\frac{4}{4}$ time is played at exceedingly slow tempos so that eighth-note rhythms on the hi-hat are not totally appropriate. This page, therefore, will offer some basic rock beats which can be used when the music is too slow to play simply a eighth-note rhythm. Notice that all the beats employ a steady sixteenth-note rhythm on the hi-hat, played with the right stick.

The next group of beats continues with steady sixteenth notes on the hi-hat. This time, however, the rhythm is played with an *alternate sticking* rather than just the right hand. In other words, play right stick, left stick, right stick, left stick, *etc.* This allows a steady sixteenth-note beat to be used at moderate tempos instead of just slow tempos, as was shown on the previous page. The beats here are extremely useful in disco drumming. Play the hi-hat rhythm on closed cymbals. After you become familiar with each beat, try opening and closing the hi-hat in different spots. Notice that the snare and hi-hat are no longer played together.

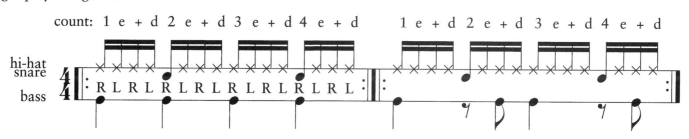

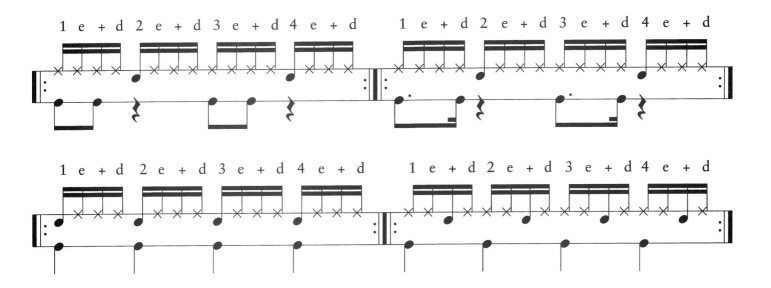

Rock Breaks

By this time you have played through a wealth of material. If you mastered each of the beats on the previous pages you will be able to play along and keep time with just about any rock group.

Pages 39 through 41 will be devoted to rock *breaks* or *fills*. Each break is presented on the third or fourth beat of the bar, and in order to keep the page as uncluttered as possible I have omitted a bass drum part. You can play the bass in any way you feel comfortable. One other point—I suggest you play one bar of an ad-lib rock rhythm before each of the written bars containing a break. This will mean that the break will come at the end of every second bar, which is much more realistic as far as actual performance is concerned. All the breaks are to be played on the snare drum.

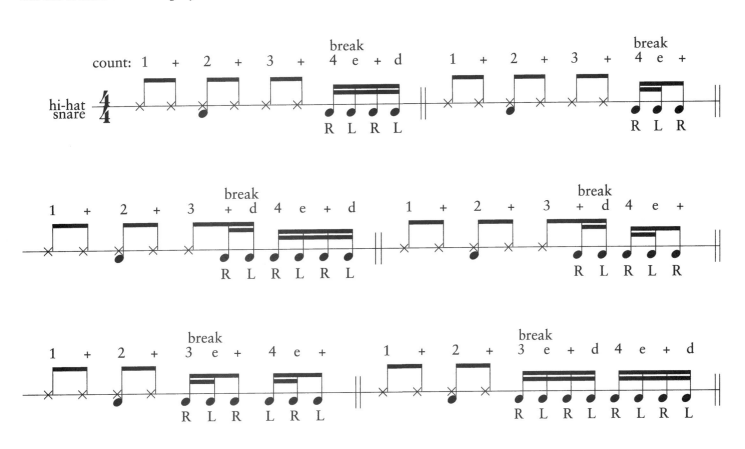

More Rock Breaks

Remember: Precede each break with one full bar of an ad-lib rock rhythm.

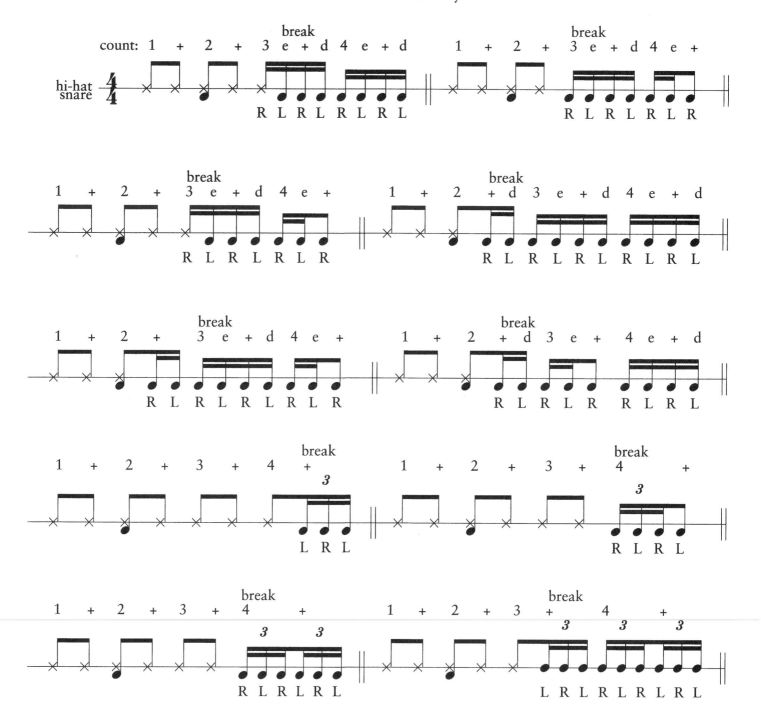

Rock Breaks around the Drums

I have selected some of the breaks from the previous page, and notated them between the snare and tom toms. This page merely provides a taste of some of the possibilities for playing breaks between the various drums, and I suggest you try to create some patterns on your own. Remember to play your bass in any manner you choose.

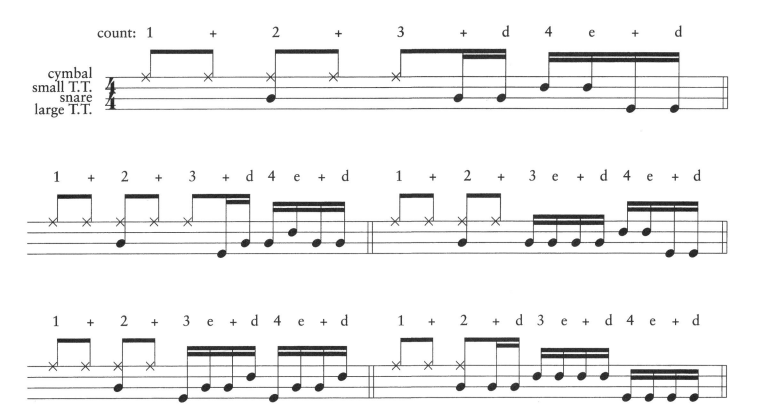

Note: T.T. means Tom-Tom.

Care of Your Kit

Keeping your kit in tip-top condition may not make you play better, but practically every good drummer I know takes pride in seeing to it that proper care is given to his instrument. When it comes to selling or trading in your kit for a new one, you'll always get a good price if it looks good. No one wants to purchase a kit that's faded, chipped, and generally in a rundown condition. The fact is that second-hand drums are always in demand, especially with inflation and the rising cost of new equipment. So, maintain your kit in as good a condition as possible, and when the time comes you'll have little difficulty selling it, perhaps even at a profit.

It's relatively easy to make your set look good. Most music stores sell special cleaners to make your cymbals shine. The same holds true for the chrome on your drums. And from time to time a good wipe down of the shells is in order. They tend to gather dust which will dull the finish if it's not wiped away.

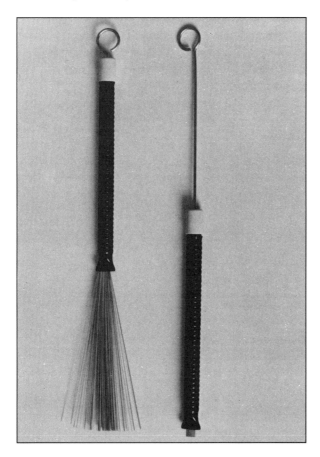

One final word about brushes. When not in use be certain to pull back the wires into their sheath. The wires bend easily, and once this happens it's difficult to get a smooth-sounding "swish" on the drumheads, causing you unnecessary expense for new brushes.

If you keep the kit set up in your home, I suggest you take the cymbals off their stands and put them away until you're ready to use them. When a cymbal is mounted it's not difficult to bump into it accidentally, knocking the entire stand over and causing the cymbal to possibly crack when it hits the floor. In fact I did just that with a favorite cymbal of mine. Besides having to purchase a new one, I've never been able to find another cymbal with quite that tone which I liked so much, since every cymbal has a unique tone. Incidentally, if you want to practice on the kit and keep the noise down, simply put some tape on the cymbal. This will stop it from vibrating and cut down its sound considerably.

Now that your cymbals are put away, cover the drums with a sheet. This will protect them from dust. Also, people who come into the house often want to bang on the drums out of curiosity. You can't blame them, but if you don't want that to happen, a covering sheet will keep the actual drums somewhat out of sight, lessening the likelihood that friends or relatives will have a go. Out of sight, out of mind.

The drumheads, of course, are the most vulnerable to wear and tear. I always see to it that the top head of the snare drum is covered with a round rubber practice pad that fits precisely over the head and under the rim. These pads are relatively inexpensive, and they afford terrific protection for the snare head. Moreover, the pad itself is quite useful to practice on when you have to keep the noise level down. Years ago drumheads were made from calf skins, which were easily affected by the weather. With the advent of plastic heads, however, the weather has little effect, so you can tune your drums once or twice during the evening, and not worry about the humidity.

The snare and accessories are generally packed into a fiberglass case, which affords excellent protection. Cases for the tom toms are either soft (made from cloth or leather) or hard (made from fiberglass). The hard cases are bulky and difficult to store but, without a doubt, they keep the drums in the best condition. The soft cases are certainly much better than nothing, but it's still easy to dent and scratch the shells when the drums are being transported since they tend to be handled roughly.

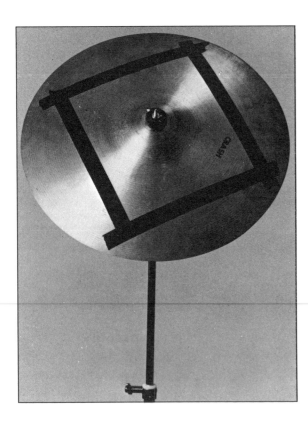